Adventures in Art

Studio Masters

3

Davis Publications, Inc. Worcester, Massachusetts

Introduction

This set of 18 Studio Masters can be **photocopied,** as needed, for classroom use. Each master provides step-by-step instructions for the prevalent studio techniques in *Adventures in Art.* They serve as technique reminders and allow students to undertake projects without the fear of damaging their books. They can become part of a student's art journal or **portfolio,** or can be **sent home** to share with parents.

These masters are intended to be used with the active participation and guidance of the teacher, in conjunction with a fully-developed lesson plan in art. While they can be used at home to finish a project, they are not intended to be used as stand-alone lessons.

The numbered statements are step-by-step directions for the student. They provide **suggestions and questions to consider** as students generate, develop, and explore their own ideas. The guidelines are general principles to be followed, **not formulas** to be strictly adhered to.

At the end of each master is a section called "Reflect," in which students are asked to look at their finished work and consider formal qualities. The questions are intended as a guide to **self-evaluation,** and reinforce the notion of craftsmanship.

The simple illustrations that accompany each master provide examples for the student. Students should be encouraged to **generate their own ideas,** not to copy or to color the examples themselves.

Correlations to *Adventures in Art* lessons are provided at the bottom of each master, and in the chart on page iv.

© 1998
Davis Publications, Inc.
Worcester, Massachusetts USA

0-87192-366-1
 2 3 4 5 6 7 8 9 10 JCO 01 00

Front cover: Student artwork by Holly Dyer, Bethel-Tate School, Bethel, Ohio. From the Crayola® Dream-Makers® Collection, courtesy of Binney & Smith, Inc.

Table of Contents

MASTER #   MASTER TITLE

	You can...	Tú puedes...
1	work with pastels	trabajar con pasteles
2	make prints of stencils	hacer grabados con matrices
3	cut many of one shape	cortar muchas figuras iguales
4	make a tissue paper collage	crear un collage con papel de seda
5	make a monoprint	crear un monograbado
6	print with clay stamps	imprimir con sellos de arcilla
7	use paint	usar pintura
8	make and use a viewfinder	crear y usar un visor
9	make a relief print	crear un grabado en relieve
10	make a resist painting	crear una pintura indeleble
11	have fun with lettering	divertirte con las letras
12	make a book	hacer un libro
13	make paper forms	crear formas de papel
14	design fabric	diseñar telas
15	make a batik design	hacer un diseño de batik
16	work with fibers	hacer un aplique
17	make a clay figure	trabajar con arcilla
18	make a paper sculpture	hacer una escultura de papel

Correlations to *Adventures in Art*

Name _____ Date _____

You can work with pastels.

1 Make different marks.

Use the tip.

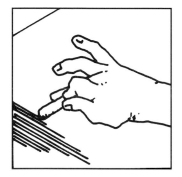

Use the side.

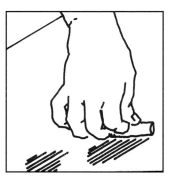

Use the end.

2 Put one color on top of another.

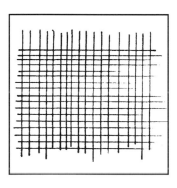

3 Blend colors.

Tissue

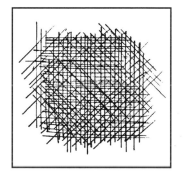

Swab

4 Reflect: How many ways did you use your pastels?

Adventures in Art, Lessons 2, 3, 11, 12, 18, 19, R2, R3

Nombre _____ Fecha _____

Tú puedes trabajar con pasteles.

1 Haz diferentes marcas.

Usa la punta.

Usa el lado.

Usa la base.

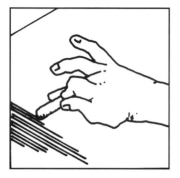

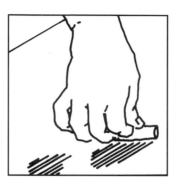

2 Pon un color sobre otro.

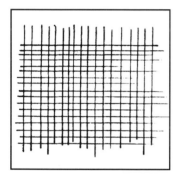

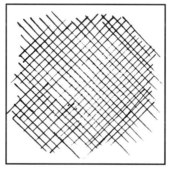

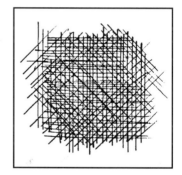

3 Mezcla los colores. Pañuelo de papel

Puntita de algodón

4 Reflexiona: ¿De cuántas maneras usaste los pasteles?

Adventures in Art, Lecciones 2, 3, 11, 12, 18, 19, R2, R3

Name _____ Date _____

You can make prints of stencils.

1 Make a stencil. Cut a shape from the center of a stiff piece of paper.

2 Place the stencil on paper. Dip a sponge brush in tempera. Dab the paint inside the cut-out shape.

3 Move your stencil and print the shape again.

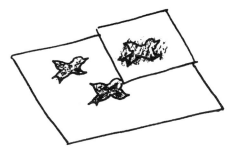

4 Reflect: Do your printed shapes have smooth edges?

Adventures in Art, Lessons 4, 5, 58

Nombre _____ Fecha _____

Tú puedes hacer grabados con matrices.

1 Haz una matriz. Recorta una figura en el centro de un trozo de papel duro.

2 Coloca la matriz sobre una hoja de papel. Moja una esponjita en témpera. Frota la pintura dentro de la figura recortada.

3 Traslada la matriz e imprime de nuevo la figura.

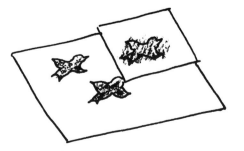

4 Reflexiona: ¿Tienen tus figuras los contornos bien definidos?

Adventures in Art, Lecciones 4, 5, 58

Name _____ Date _____

You can cut many of one shape.

For many of one shape in one color

1 Fold paper in half. Then fold it in half again.

2 Cut your shape.

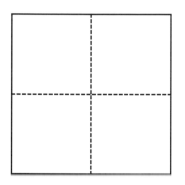

For many of one shape in many colors

1 Clip four colors of paper together.

2 Cut your shape.

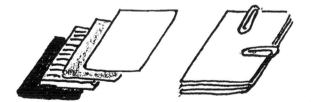
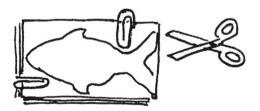

Reflect: What patterns can you make with your shapes?

Adventures in Art, Lessons 6, 39, 40

Nombre _____ Fecha _____

Tú puedes cortar muchas figuras iguales.

Para muchas figuras iguales del mismo color

1 Dobla una hoja de papel por la mitad. Luego vuélvela a doblar por la mitad.

2 Recorta tu figura.

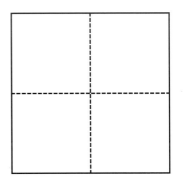

Para muchas figuras iguales de distintos colores

1 Sujeta con un clip cuatro hojas de papel de distintos colores.

2 Recorta tu figura.

Reflexiona: ¿Qué patrones puedes crear con tus figuras?

Adventures in Art, Lecciones 6, 39, 40

Name _____ Date _____

You can make a tissue paper collage.

1 Plan your design.

2 Cut or tear colored tissue paper.

3 Brush glue on the background. Arrange tissue pieces.

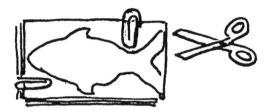

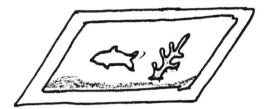

4 Brush glue on the arrangement. Add more shapes.

5 Brush glue over the finished work.

6 Reflect: What happens when you overlap shapes?

Nombre _____ Fecha _____

Tú puedes crear un collage con papel de seda.

1 Planea tu diseño.

2 Corta o rasga una hoja de papel de seda de color.

3 Aplica pegamento en la parte de atrás. Coloca las figuras de papel de seda.

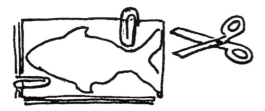

4 Aplica pegamento sobre las figuras. Añade más figuras.

5 Aplica pegamento sobre el trabajo ya terminado.

6 Reflexiona: ¿Qué sucede cuando superpones figuras?

Adventures in Art, Lecciones 7, 42, 46

Name _____ Date _____

You can make a monoprint.

1 Brush tempera on a smooth plastic or metal surface.

2 Create a design in the wet paint. Use swabs, cotton balls, facial tissue, or a stick.

3 Place paper over the wet paint. Rub the paper all over.

4 Pull up the paper.

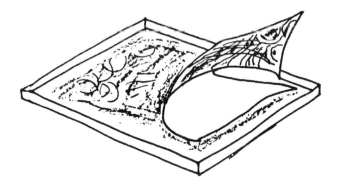

5 Reflect: Does your design show clearly?

Adventures in Art, Lesson 9

Nombre _____ Fecha _____

Tú puedes crear un monograbado.

1 Aplica témpera sobre una superficie lisa de metal o de plástico.

2 Crea un diseño sobre la pintura húmeda. Usa puntitas de algodón, bolas de algodón, pañuelos de papel o un palito.

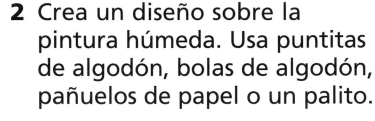

3 Coloca una hoja de papel sobre la pintura húmeda. Frota toda la superficie de la hoja.

4 Levanta la hoja de papel.

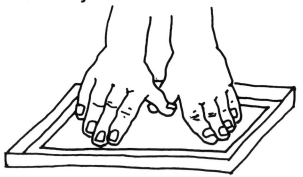

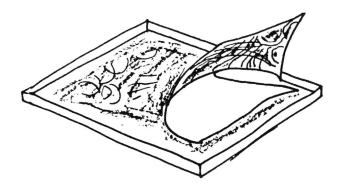

5 Reflexiona: ¿Se ve tu diseño con claridad?

Adventures in Art, Lección 9

Name _____ Date _____

You can print with clay stamps.

1 Make clay forms.

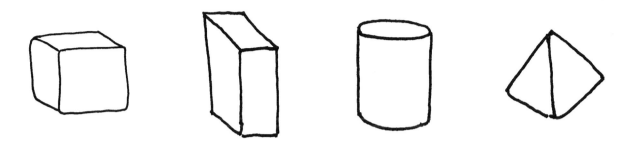

2 Use a pencil, stick, or small object. Press a design in a flat side.

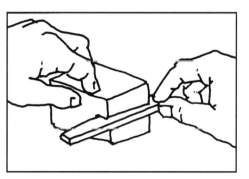

3 Press your stamp on a stamp pad. Print it on paper.

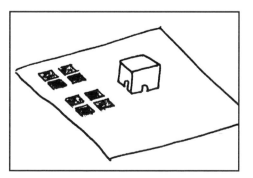

4 Reflect: Did your design print clearly? Why or why not?

Adventures in Art, Lesson 10

Nombre _____   Fecha _____

Tú puedes imprimir con sellos de arcilla.

1 Modela formas de arcilla.

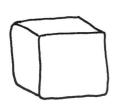 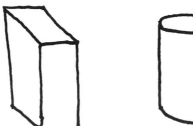 

2 Usa un lápiz, un palito o un objeto pequeño. Presiona un diseño sobre un lado plano.

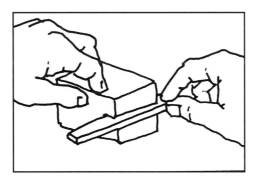

3 Presiona tu sello sobre tinta. Imprímelo sobre papel.

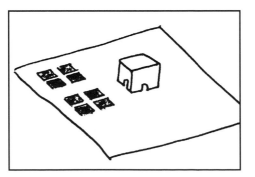

4 Reflexiona: ¿Se te imprimió el diseño con claridad? ¿Por qué?

Adventures in Art, Lección 10

Name _____ Date _____

You can use paint.

| Wash | Wipe | Blot | Next color |

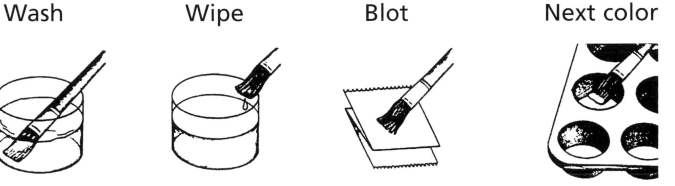

Mix tints and shades

Tints: Mix a dot of color with white paint.

Shades: Mix a dot of black with a color.

Mix colors

Red + yellow = orange

Red + blue = violet

Yellow + blue = green

Reflect: Did you try mixing colors, tints, and shades?

Adventures in Art, Lessons 13, 14, 15, 17, 20, 27

Nombre _____ Fecha _____

Tú puedes usar pintura.

Enjuaga	Escurre	Seca	Otro color

Mezcla matices y sombras

Matices: Mezcla una puntita de color con pintura blanca.

Sombras: Mezcla una puntita de negro con un color.

Mezcla colores

Rojo + amarillo = naranja
Rojo + azul = violeta
Amarillo + azul = verde

Reflexiona: ¿Intentaste mezclar colores, matices y sombras?

Name _____ Date _____

You can make and use a viewfinder.

1 Fold and cut a viewfinder.

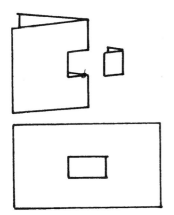

2 Find a scene to draw.

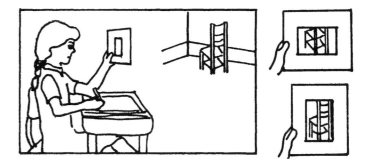

3 Look from different positions.

4 Draw what you see.

5 Reflect: How many views of a scene can you make?

Adventures in Art, Lessons U2, 16, 24

Nombre _____ Fecha _____

Tú puedes crear y usar un visor.

1 Dobla y corta un visor.

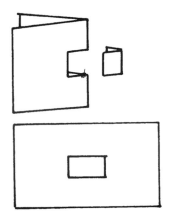

2 Busca una escena que quieras dibujar.

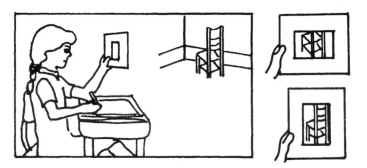

3 Mira desde distintas posiciones.

4 Dibuja lo que ves.

5 Reflexiona: ¿Cuántas vistas de una misma escena puedes hacer?

Adventures in Art, Lecciones U2, 16, 24

Name _____ Date _____

You can make a relief print.

1 Shape a clay slab with your hands. Make a thick, smooth block.

2 Draw your design. Carve it into the clay.

3 Brush paint on the flat parts of the block.

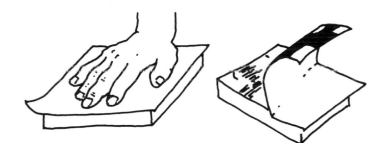

4 Pul paper on the block. Rub it gently. Lift the paper.

5 Reflect: Did your design print clearly?

Adventures in Art, Lesson 22

Nombre _____ Fecha _____

Tú puedes crear un grabado en relieve.

1 Modela un bloque de arcilla con las manos. Crea un bloque grueso y liso.

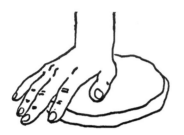

2 Dibuja tu diseño. Tállalo en la arcilla.

3 Pinta con un pincel las partes planas del bloque.

4 Coloca una hoja de papel sobre el bloque. Frota con suavidad. Levanta la hoja.

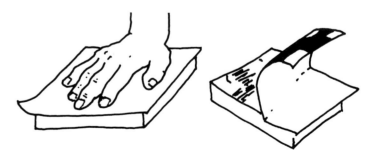

5 Reflexiona: ¿Se te imprimió el diseño con claridad?

Name _____ Date _____

You can make a resist painting.

1 Outline shapes with crayon or oil pastels.

2 Color in some areas.
Leave some areas blank.
Use bright colors.
Press hard.

3 Brush paint over the entire paper.

4 Reflect: Did the paint roll away from the crayon in all areas?

Adventures in Art, Lessons 30, 41

Nombre _____ Fecha _____

Tú puedes crear una pintura indeleble.

1 Dibuja el contorno de varias figuras con crayones o pasteles.

2 Colorea algunas áreas.
Deja otras en blanco.
Usa colores vivos.
Aprieta fuerte.

3 Pinta con un pincel toda la hoja.

4 Reflexiona: ¿Resabló la pintura por todas las áreas del crayón?

Adventures in Art, Lecciones 30, 41

Name _____ Date _____

You can have fun with lettering.

Use the guidelines on this page. Or, change the letters into objects, plants, or animals.

Reflect: Are all your letters readable?

Nombre _____   Fecha _____

Tú puedes divertirte con las letras.

Usa estas letras de guía. O, transforma las letras en objetos, plantas o animales.

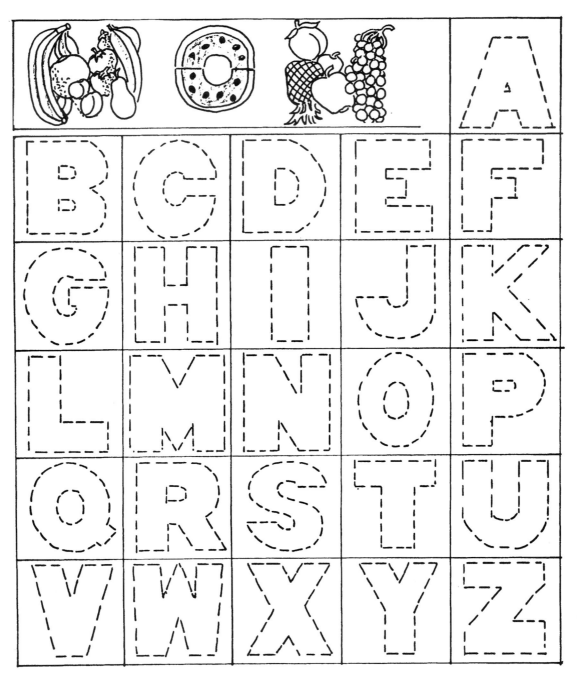

Reflexiona: ¿Se leen bien todas tus letras?

Adventures in Art, Lecciones 32, 34

Name _____ Date _____

You can make a book.

1 Fold a narrow flap on one end of several sheets of paper.

2 Fold the other end up to the flap.

3 Apply glue to the inside of each flap and join the sheets together.

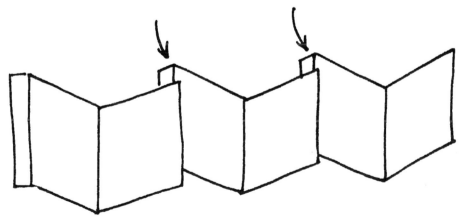

4 Reflect: Are the edges of your book straight?

Adventures in Art, Lesson 35

Nombre _____ Fecha _____

Tú puedes hacer un libro.

1 Haz un doblez pequeño en un extremo de varias hojas de papel.

2 Dobla el otro extremo hacia el doblez.

3 Aplica pegamento en la parte interior de cada doblez y une las hojas.

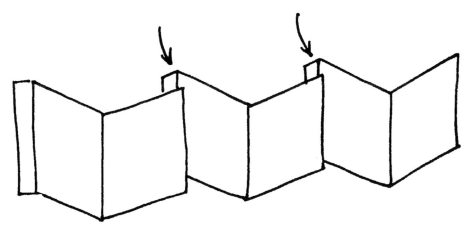

4 Reflexiona: ¿Están rectos los bordes de tu libro?

Adventures in Art, Lección 35

Name _____ Date _____

You can make paper forms.

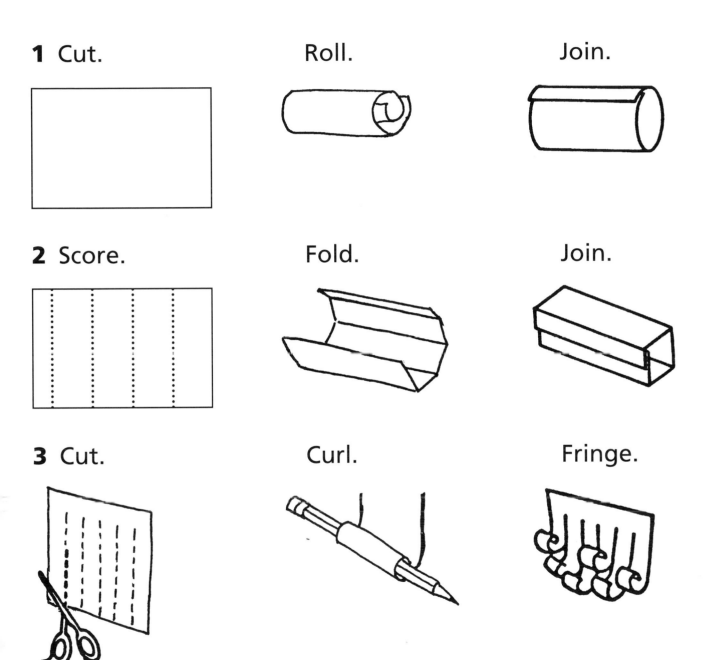

1 Cut.   Roll.   Join.

2 Score.   Fold.   Join.

3 Cut.   Curl.   Fringe.

4 Reflect: What paper forms did you use in your artwork?

Adventures in Art, Lessons 43, 54

Nombre _____   Fecha _____

Tú puedes crear formas de papel.

1 Recorta.   Enrolla.   Une.

2 Marca.   Dobla.   Une.

3 Recorta.   Riza.   Haz flecos.

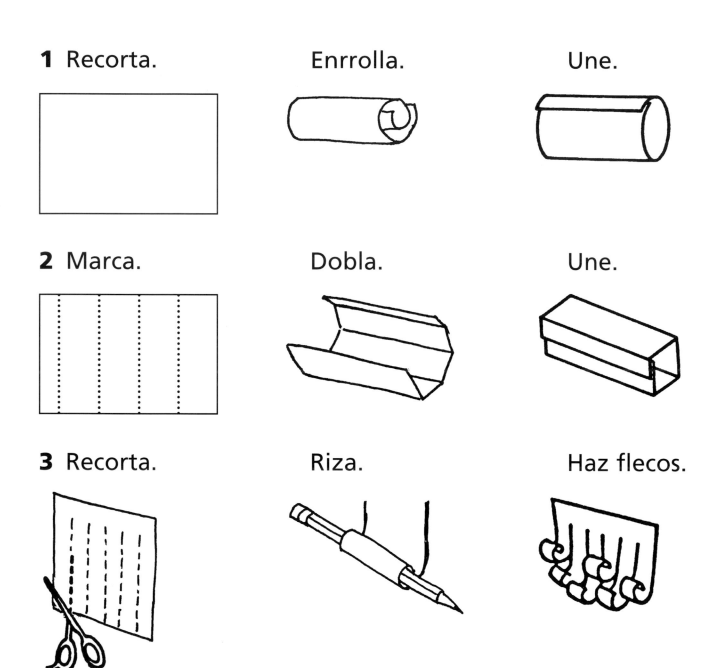

4 Reflexiona: ¿Qué formas de papel usaste en tu obra?

Adventures in Art, Lecciones 43, 54

Name _____   Date _____

You can design fabric.

1 Start with a piece of burlap. Draw a line along the four sides. Make a fringe outside the lines.

2 Create a pattern. Pull out some threads. Leave some of these spaces empty.

3 Add new threads. Weave different colors of yarn over and under the burlap threads.

4 Reflect: Did you weave your new threads evenly into the burlap?

Adventures in Art, Lesson 50

Nombre _____ Fecha _____

Tú puedes diseñar telas.

1 Empieza con un pedazo de tela de saco. Dibuja una línea a lo largo de los cuatro lados. Haz un fleco por la parte exterior de las líneas.

2 Crea un diseño. Estira algunos hilos. Deja vacíos algunos de estos espacios.

3 Añade nuevos hilos. Teje hilo de distintos colores por encima y por debajo de los hilos de la tela de saco.

4 Reflexiona: ¿Tejiste los nuevos hilos uniformemente por la tela de saco?

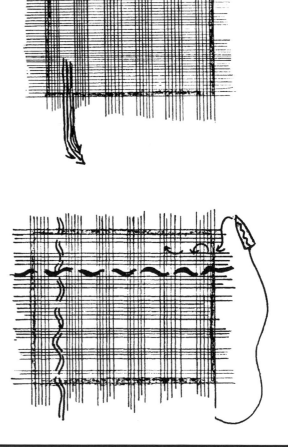

Adventures in Art, Lección 50

Name _____ Date _____

You can make a batik design.

1 Make a paper stencil.

2 Place the stencil on white cloth. Brush resist medium inside the stencil cutout. Move the stencil to another area and apply more medium.

3 When the medium is dry, brush tempera paint over the whole cloth.

4 Use running water. Wash out the medium.

5 Reflect: Is your design easy to see?

Adventures in Art, Lesson 51

Nombre _____   Fecha _____

Tú puedes hacer un diseño de batik.

1 Haz una matriz de papel.

2 Coloca la matriz sobre tela blanca. Aplica un material indeleble dentro de la matriz recortada. Traslada la matriz a otro espacio y haz lo mismo.

3 Cuando el medio se seque, aplica témpera sobre toda la tela.

4 Usa agua del grifo. Retira el material.

5 Reflexiona: ¿Es tu diseño fácil de ver?

Adventures in Art, Lección 51

Name _____ Date _____

You can make an appliqué.

1 Cut shapes out of cloth.

2 Arrange them on a cloth background.

3 Dab with glue to hold pieces in place.

4 Stitch shapes to the background.

5 Reflect: Did you stitch around the edges of your shapes? Are the stitches even?

Adventures in Art, Lesson 52

Nombre _____   Fecha _____

Tú puedes hacer un aplique.

1 Recorta figuras de tela.

2 Colócalas sobre un fondo también de tela.

3 Sujeta las figuras sobre la tela con pegamento.

4 Cose las figuras a la tela del fondo.

5 Reflexiona: ¿Cosiste tus figuras por los bordes? ¿Son las puntadas iguales?

Name _____ Date _____

You can work with clay.

Join

Press separate parts together.
Blend joints with X strokes.

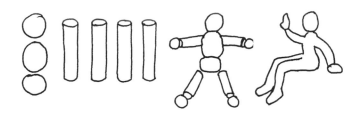

Make coils

Bend, pinch, and join to shape.

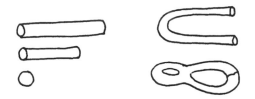

Carve

Draw your design on a
cylinder. Carve slowly.

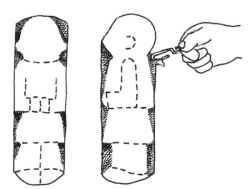

Relief

Draw your design on a slab.
Carve away some background.

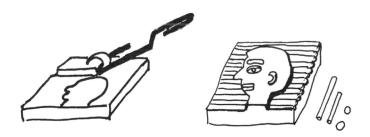

Reflect: Did you add or subtract clay to make your sculpture?

Adventures in Art, Lessons 53, 56, 57, 58

Nombre _____   Fecha _____

Tú puedes trabajar con arcilla.

Une

Junta distintas partes presionándolas. Une las juntas haciendo X con el dedo.

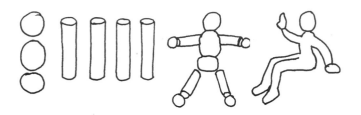

Haz rollos

Curva, pellizca y une dándoles forma.

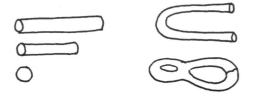

Talla

Dibuja tu diseño en un cilindro. Talla bien despacio.

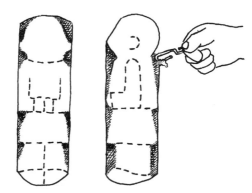

Crea relieve

Dibuja tu diseño sobre un bloque. Quita arcilla del fondo.

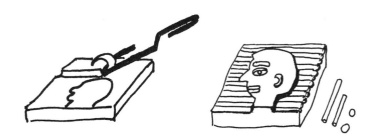

Reflexiona: ¿Añadiste o quitaste arcilla para crear tu escultura?

Adventures in Art, Lecciones 53, 56, 57, 58

Name _____   Date _____

You can make a paper sculpture.

1 Draw a big shape on folded paper. Add color to your drawing.

2 Cut the folded paper. Add color to the other side.

3 Glue some edges. Leave the bottom open.

4 Stuff crumpled paper inside. Glue the bottom.

5 Reflect: Does your sculpture look the same on both sides?

Adventures in Art, Lesson 55

Nombre _____ Fecha _____

Tú puedes hacer una escultura de papel.

1 Dibuja una figura grande sobre una hoja de papel doblado. Añade color a tu dibujo.

2 Recorta la hoja de papel doblado. Añade color a la otra parte.

3 Pega algunos extremos. Deja la base abierta.

4 Introduce papeles arruga-dos por la abertura. Pega la base.

5 Reflexiona: ¿Es tu figura igual por ambos lados?

Adventures in Art, Lección 55